Like Vapor

To Jim and Linda

Like Vapor
Joy Gaines-Friedler

Mayapple Press 2008

Published by   MAYAPPLE PRESS
                    408 N. Lincoln St.
                    Bay City, MI 48708
                    www.mayapplepress.com

ISBN 978-932412-65-2

ACKNOWLEDGMENTS

The Litchfield Review: A Lesson About Boys, Another Field, Communion, The Arboretum, Walking Away; *Swallow The Moon:* Eve, How We Love Our Parents, She Actually Became My Friend, And Then This; *Hazmet* and First Place Walrus Press Contest 2004: Welfare In America; *Lilliput Review:* Yes, It's a Love Poem; *Driftwood Review:* The Love Poems of Anne Sexton; *Rattle:* Assisted Living; *Albatrose:* Row Boat; *MARGIE:* Capitalism South Carolina; *Pebble Lake Review:* Anger.

I would like to thank my teachers from Oakland Community College and Oakland University, including Fd Hara, Peter Stine, David James, Gladys Cardiff, Maureen Dunphy, Susan Hawkins, and Annie Gilson.

I would also like to thank Mary Ann Samyn, an amazing poet and teacher, Director of Far Field Writer's Retreat, without which, I would not have had the opportunity to work with so many incredible poets and teachers of poetry.

Also, a special thanks to poet and teacher, Mary Jo Firth Gillett, whose workshops the entire Detroit area literary community covets. And a thank you to John D. Lamb, M.L. Liebler, and all the other folks at Springfed Arts that allow this community voice and place.

I would like to thank my friends, especially my Friday tennis group, and family, for putting up with spontaneous readings and near nervous breakdowns. And lastly, I want to thank my husband Moti; without Moti none of this would have been possible.

Cover art by Joy Gaines-Friedler. Cover designed by Judith Kerman. Photograph of Joy Gaines-Friedler by Moti Friedler. Book typeset by Amee Schmidt with text in Californian FB and titles in Mirror thin.

Contents

Section I

Bad Dog	3
First Light	4
A Lesson About Boys	5
At Hart Plaza	6
A Blind Man Peddles Pencils...	7
The House Around the Corner	8
Assisted Living	9
Domestic Violence	10
After	11
She Actually Became My Friend	12
The Unknown Woman in Vincent's Room	13
Too Much Yes	14
Grief	15

Section II

Childless Morning	19
Named New	20
Her Medicine	21
Like Vapor	22
Distracted Angels	23
At the Kitchen Sink	24
Anger	25
While Dad Recovers from Surgery	26
How We Love Our Parents	27
Broken Rose	28
Flight	29
A Pheasant Is Crossing I-75 North of Grayling	30
Damn This Plane Heading South	31
Talking to My Father on the Phone...	32
Walking Away	33
The Arboretum	34
And Then This	35
Communion	36

Section III

Redemption on Bus 18—Bat Yam to Tel Aviv   41
Detroit   42
Eastern Market   43
Corners   44
Blink   45
Rosabelle   46
"No Kidding...You Play Too?"   47
Capitalism South Carolina   48
Eve   50
Yes, It's a Love Poem   51
The Love Poems of Anne Sexton   52
Welfare in America   53
Row Boat   54
Another Field   55

Section I

Understanding you can be
unhappy and still be content,
isn't that the beginning of wisdom?

—Gladys Cardiff

Bad Dog

Mom was still in her robe when the bell rang.
I was five. It was summer. There was a cop at the door.

I stood next to my mother on the front porch
as the officer explained why he was writing

yet another ticket: Blackie had gotten out again.
A lady complained that he molested her French Poodle,

and can't we do something about that dog.
No sir, thank you sir, sorry sir,

and the cop left. Mom turned to open the front door.

We were locked out. She rang the bell.
I remember my father yelling from inside,

someone's at the door, answer the god-damned door.
Mom rang the bell, and rang that bell.

She said, *shit.* She pulled her robe in closer,
angry at dad, angry at Blackie,

and I felt her anger fall all over me.
I knew that I could easily climb through the milk chute.

I knew, even then, that I would have to save her.

First Light

This is the hour before the wind,
before watering, winning, oil,
cans, gas cans, core issues, clanking
cacophony. Before the word *country*.
This is the hour when mallards stir,
clear throats, click, cluck, shake,
eye thistle and corn at the feeders,
eye tadpoles, float, feed, paddle, pluck.
This is the hour before the sun
has risen over the edge
of arborvitae and spruce, before
daylilies open in its heat,
before another desperate blast
from the hill, noise drummed out
because we can't stand to hear
the hum of vehemence, another
frame, a roving band of framers,
forging, marching, for the sake
of what? for what? for what? This is
the hour before *foreign* and *freedom*,
before dressing, pressing cults
and sects, before suicide, walls,
mortar, motors, employ, deploy.
This is the hour before thirst,
before belts and vests, before prayer
and martyrdom. This is the hour
before breakfast, buses and bones,
backpacks, brigadiers, before nails
and bits of metal, before redeploying
cell phones, web sites, framers.
This is the hour before refilling the feeders.

A Lesson About Boys

As a kid I learned science from my brother
who turned the sun on innocent ants
and fried them with a magnifying glass.

I liked the effect—sun as source, glass as catalyst—
but I could never bring myself to vaporize
a living creature *because it's so cool.*

Later, he got into trouble at school
for smacking a kid on the back of the head
as he leaned over the drinking fountain,

the kid's teeth connecting with metal.
There was an issue of blood
and angry parents.

When he turned his fist toward me
I grabbed his wrist. Before we hit the ground
my brother's hands

became a system of knowledge, general truths
about boys: I learned to walk around them slowly,
be especially careful on sunny days.

At Hart Plaza

A gazelle of a child,
all legs and arms,
checks his watch
as the stream of fountain
pours over him,
his shirt and shorts
stuck to him like wet psalms.
He is a glistening pole
of wrought iron and glass.
I want to ask him
where he got that watch,
want to take him home,
hear stories about school
how he plays guard, how
he secretly cares for the younger kids.
Driving past Denby High
one three-o-clock,
I saw the police cars posted
like sentries at the corners,
saw the thin chests of boys
all heron necked
and threatening, scuttling,
a threat, a scuttle, a threat.
The houses are not theirs.
The churches embedded
with six pointed stars.
On the sidewalk a poem:
people have roaches, and act
like they don't.

A Blind Man Peddles Pencils
Outside the Walgreens
on Woodward in Royal Oak

His face wears a layer of grit.

A man who can't describe mirrors,
can't describe blue, or water,
or light—except in terms of heat
and energy.

His mother gave birth nine times,
four of her babies born blind.

He rides the bus two hours,
says he likes the customers here.

Five years. Mugged once. Faith,
when a woman from Canada
gave him fifty bucks.

How did he know?

His eyes sweep across thoughts,
as though he is always inside himself,
as though he lives inside a prayer.

He listens his way through traffic
and automatic doors. He listens
to the muted thud of change
against a yellow plastic cup.

The House Around the Corner

This is a house where no marker
designates its history, no gable
or dormer dictates its style,

nothing points to year or fathers
at war, no mothers caught
in the silence of loneliness.

There are steps and porch,
a wood pillar of peeling paint.
Ivy foams around an oak.

No one claimed injustice here.
No one begged forgiveness.
No one sought escape.

No dog left holes around the fence.
There is nothing here,
that cannot be rebuilt.

Assisted Living

A woman downstairs is speaking Spanish on a cell phone.
She hasn't taken a breath in forty minutes. Her task is to guard

the rice-pale women that sit beside her in wheelchairs asleep
in the shade. They are like the shredded skin of exotic insects.

Exquisite. They are feathers and cotton. They are kites.
They once had New Year's Eve to think about. They had lovers.

They had many shoes. Today my mother showed me pictures of herself.
It was 1944. She was black and white gorgeous, her dark eyes pillows

among the uniformed men all devilish and legible, the tenements and
walk-ups plump with community. There were no shopping malls,

no endless rows of freeway lights. There was no sorry in her eyes.
One moonlit night while my father was dying

I heard a hum of voices through the wall. It was very late.
I loved the sound of them talking. The rise of question,

the pause, the rise of answer.
They spoke in the language of walls.

As they faded from black and white to color
my father died. Now, my mother curses the deaf,

the spoor of sparrows, the blossoms that slip from the dogwood,
the memory of kisses, the thing that lifts the wind.

Domestic Violence

The mauve couch in the family room
where she sat folding laundry

watching television with her mother.
The door he entered with the key

he had not yet relinquished.
The argument no one will recall.

The gun he bought that day at K-Mart.
The hole through the couch she barely

escaped. The second in the door frame
of the kitchen where she reached

the phone, pushed 911 on speed dial. Her mother's
hands that grabbed his arm. The way he shook them off.

The explosion that cracked through the ceiling
and spit bits of plaster and yellow paint.

The fourth blast that scored a bullet seared gouge
across the innocent linoleum, shattering floor molding.

The kitchen table she tried to wear as a shield.
The sour smell of gunpowder.

Two more holes
from the rounds none of us will escape.

After

I sat on the porch swing listening to the bees
praying in the lilacs. I thought of that scar

carved into her forehead. She told me
a box fell from a shelf in the garage.

I tried to remember what she said the day before.
She said, *he is sick.* She said, *leaving,* and

lawyers. She said, *unlucky,* and something
about not telling her mother. She never

said that she was scared.
She never said, *restraining order.*

If only I had had the chance I would have
given him the old *if you ever... again.* We

would have told everyone about him, built
a fortress with that knowledge.

I sat on the porch swing listening to the gospel of bees,
surveyed her life, then changed the ending.

She Actually Became My Friend

When I met her she was working the popcorn machine
at the Detroit Jazz Festival. She gave me a
you're all about the suburbs look
while she reached her hand into Plexiglas
and reloaded the container of flavored oil.
Aiming her working class background at me
she calculated my weight
by dividing hers in half, then asked "what size?"
If I said, "give me a large with butter,"
she'd think, *that bitch can eat whatever she wants
and still stay thin.* If I said, "small please,"
I was certain to get an *uh huh,*
and a confirmation that I am a puny-assed wimp.
I asked for a medium,
then commented on the number of teenagers at the show,
told her how at sixteen I was busy cleaning the common areas
of an apartment complex, skipping school, fighting
with my boyfriend, and wallowing in The Moody Blues.
I felt like a hostage negotiator wearing down angry resolve.
Years later, while discussing the music of Palistrina's Mass,
and self-indulgent in our own literary obesity,
I asked her about that day.
She said I looked like the kind that surrounded
myself with appliances and kept my cats indoors.
She said, she would never do it—raise a kid in the suburbs—
and that for her, remaining poor is a thread to God.
She said that glass tumbled in a chamber
becomes a kaleidoscope of shape and pattern.
The suburbs, she said, are the colorless pieces.

The Unknown Woman
in Vincent's Room

I've made it mine.
My picture hangs with woven threads
of Dutch hide on violet walls.
A portrait of you, Vincent, hangs next to my bed.
(I have also made you my best friend.)
You claim the floor is red tile,
I say wood, but we've had this argument before.
You own the colors.
Despite me, you changed them three times.
That is what I love about you, Vincent,
the yellow rebel of you—your refusal to use white.
You feel the subtle difference
between lilac doors and violet walls.
My bed—you are welcome to share it—
has two citron-green pillows and a madly vermilion blanket.
It blocks the door, but not enough that you can't go out,
or return anytime you want.
Besides, there is that other blue door you like to use.
Your friend Bosch ran off with his portrait
that hung in this version of your bedroom.
I was tired of it myself.
When you replaced it with that strange bearded soldier,
I begged you to get rid of it, too. You did.
Now the third version contains a portrait of me.
How nice.
But you need your quiet, Vincent.
You need to escape the rounded shoulders of sunflowers,
and the voices you hear in yellow cafes.
I've closed the solid shutters, suppressing shadows
(like those Japanese prints you love.)
I like the intimacy it creates.

Too Much Yes

Where is that part of *no*
that forms at the mouth
so sure of itself

it can beat up the boys?

Laid down like a word,
a broken tree limb,
like a blackout.

Something lives at the end of *no*.
Something, not like a flower,
but rather, like the moon.

Solid. Concrete. Immovable.

Grief

My grief goes with me
like the friends I've lost.
Comforting to know
that it is here.
I call on sorrow
to remind me
that life is not
external or hollow,
but rather full
of content
in moments
that only sorrow
can awaken in me.
I call on grief
to rouse my suspicion,
arrest complacency,
repair my passion,
embrace my gladness.
Grief escapes from me,
I catch it, I wear it
like a warm winter coat
feeling its brave weight
restore me again.
I call on sorrow
to keep me quiet,
to touch my memories,
to reunite me
with my friends.

Section II

I like when he colors with me.

—a five year old speaking about her father

Childless Morning

This morning the air finds this way
to travel as though it is a man—old—
and has earned its forgetful pace.

It is a cat inventing new words,
something to do with *lap*,
and *now*, and *why not*?

I think about the children I never had,
the child I never drove in the back seat
telling stories about my day.

I have no use for back seats.

The wind is the air that moves
because the earth moves,

and in between its purrs and complaints comes
a recurring sound of cars.
A cat tries to get on my lap for the third time.

I nudge him away. He finds his basket
and leaves me fur in my coffee.
Isn't something always left behind?

The way thistle attaches itself to blue jeans,
oil polka-dots the garage floor,
that thing left over that is not a thing,
but rather a sense,

when tiny fingers wrap around yours.

Named New

My friend Heather is good at biting.
Her name is the color of perfume. Her clothes
stink of leather. She is the back seat of a Chevy
way too clean to really be hers.
She is the daughter of names like Fat Boy
and Dog Face. Heather wishes she were someone else
and wears a different hair style every month.
Like going to a mikvah. Like baptism.
Like past-life-therapy. I walk around in my name
trying to escape its implications,
trying to live up to its expectations.
In sixth grade I won an award for Miss Congeniality.
I had no idea of its meaning.
Later, it made sense because my name
told them to, and because Debbie Chareley
was so badly made fun of. It didn't seem so
hard to be kind. Maybe kindness bleeds
into the color of names, making them purple
and orange. It fades out too. Like a sun burnt rug.
I want to grow a new name.
Like Cassius Clay. Like a nun. Like my friend Karen
who changed her name to Julianna and remarried
her ex-husband Ed who renamed himself Willowbei.
Where did they come up with those names?
Karen says Julianna is her real name.
Imagine coming home one day knowing that,
feeling the green and gold of that. My friend
Steve went to the movies and came home Zechariah.
We were eighteen. He says he liked the color.
I thought it was the acid he dropped.
Maybe it made him feel like rain.

Her Medicine

Today I inched my way toward
the sound of a woman's confession
at the checkout counter
   ...my beautiful daughter...
as if reaching toward bus diesel
streets, cast iron grates, broken
fragments of glass,
   ...committed suicide.
Confession at the checkout counter
in a store that sells Hallmark cards
and creamy ceramic baskets filled
with plastic pastel eggs, Anita Baker
singing You Bring Me Joy.
I inched my way closer, wanting
to hear more about the kids
who *couldn't find their mother.*
Her voice a plea, then silent
as the float of space after a siren.
Someone asked what happened.
We gathered around her, offering
sacred herb and sweet grass, hoping
to be her medicine. We circled her. Strangers
in a Hallmark store handing her what we could.

Like Vapor

My mother is the cloud's
misty edges.
Soon she will disappear.
      Again,

I draw her with color pencil,
white pencil on white
paper,
      gray on gray.

She is the fog that hovers
above the quiet water

dissolved by sunlight
at dawn.

Distracted Angels

An angel assigned to me is day-dreaming.
She files her nails, chews on Juicy Fruit,
and makes up names for herself in Spanish; can't
decide between Chiquita and Sylvester;
she's pretty sure Sylvester is Spanish.
An angel assigned to me listens to the wind chimes
outside my bedroom, stares at the swaying
copper as one stares at fire. He seems depressed.
I tell him knock-knock jokes. He offers only mumbles.
A tiny angel in blonde curls dances in circles
to the Foreigner lyrics *Urgent, Urgent, Emergency.*
She flashes a smile and throws a pink message pad
at me with the box, *urgent,* checked off. She doesn't
remember my name and calls me "Boise."
I don't know why, except that I like potatoes
and they grow them in Idaho. An angel
assigned to me is asleep between the sound board
and the strings of my piano, flattening G when I play
Joni. One of my angels has forgotten my phone number,
can't remember my e-mail, and has become
frantic because he misplaced his reading glasses—
again. He keeps showing up at my old house,
forgetting that I moved over a year ago.
There is an angel assigned to me that won't
get out of the bathtub. He is trying different
salts: lavender, petroulli. He is so busy
relaxing that he hasn't noticed the smell of smoke,
or the insulation about to go up in flames.

At the Kitchen Sink

He said, *you're going to kill me before the cancer
does.* My mother saw no humor in that.

It filled me with something like a name,
like heritage from secrets only families know.

For a moment I forgot that I had been a refugee.

I sat at the kitchen table while he held her at the sink.
It was supposed to be me, she cried.

I swear, he said, *I'm not going anywhere.*
The moment so merciless, yet,

like an iris, or the hatching of a muscovy,
raw. Exposed.

Inside me something blossomed.

Anger

Because he was once married to a ballerina who leapt
from the Greenboro Bridge leaving him with two boys

and a girl who grew to hate his ruddy face mapped
with the tributaries of the river Drink. Maybe she heard

the words *go back* too many times, as in *go back to him.*
The slow rise and fall of the ravined river—the only breath

she could match. Anger is subtle (like something
in which you get lost and it becomes impossible

to find its beginnings.) She passed it on,
like her mother's china given to her on their wedding night,

when she first shook off a doubt that felt
like fear. *Go back.* Bravery should count for something.

While Dad Recovers from Surgery

I imagine myself in a cabin,
windows and woods, a slice of water,

and rocks that alter the flow.
I imagine my breath matching dawn,

and water not bothered by wind.
I imagine my father telling stories

about the war years and girlfriends,
and how he almost drowned once,

thinking he was in shallow water,
no footing, someone pulled him out.

I am already on the other side of his life
looking back at unasked questions.

I imagine myself by water
watching over my dad—yelling to him,

it is still too deep, keep swimming,
it is still too deep.

How We Love Our Parents

We leave a list of disasters by the telephone
in case they call:

The sump pump broke.
The basement flooded.

The garage floor is cracked.
Our circular saw was stolen.

They respond with lots of *oh-nos'*
and *oh for God's sake.*

It is how we make them happy.

Broken Rose

My mother holds it in her hand,
asks me to fix it.

I say, *I see your hands are bleeding.*
Let go. Just let it go.

My brother holds a fist at me,
I turn my back on him.

You'll be sorry when I am gone,
my father says.
I am sorry now, I tell him,

and gather twigs to use as stakes.

Flight

Up here there are streets but no houses.
There are rivers. The shore can only be imagined.
Cirrus spread thin like silk blankets.

Before I left, my father said, *hospital bed.*
I became a cold metal tray and thought of food
he will be served but will not eat.

He told me how he loves the clouds in Florida,
how they rise straight up from the land, how
sometimes he sees the face of his father in them.

In the distance dark nimbus threaten. I hold
a wooden box my father made,
run my fingers over it, smell the cedar.

A Pheasant Is Crossing I-75 North of Grayling

where the highway is a line penciled between trees.
I am changing lanes to avoid it. It is the last day
in the month of expansion,

purple iris, peony, fleshy and plump as Mae West.
Today marks one year, like pollen stain,
that my father began his lousy check marks

on a schedule of medications he cursed,
then swallowed. That bird, inching its way
across the right lane, is becoming a sparrow.

My father told me how he almost drowned
three different times. Someone always saved him.

I put Bruce Springsteen into the CD player
—*oh thunder road, oh thunder road*—
and imagine myself dancing on that porch

in a summer dress, barefoot. I would have left
with Bruce if he had asked me.
Last year, on this day, I asked my father

if I could call Hospice, get him some relief.
I'm looking at that god-forsaken bird.
I hate it for not knowing it could die.

Damn This Plane Heading South

Damn these fake leather seats
and the man who keeps coughing.
Damn the rhythm of the engines groaning,
this dry recycled air, this plastic cup of water.
Damn the discovery that I've lost an earring,
and that tumor shutting down my father's life.
Damn John Irving and Owen Meany, whom I still
cannot finish, and this journal whose pages
are dwindling. Damn the sun that burned holes
in my mother's cheek and forehead.
Damn peanut butter and jelly for its implications,
Isabella for her unrelenting
smile, my brother, my sleepy
eyes, and those lakes down there:
one looks like a stomach,
one like the state of Florida,
one looks like a penis—*Penis Lake in Dickhead, Tennesee.*
Damn that ocean of clouds that looks like choppy chunks
of frozen ground, that layer of cumulus canyons
separating me from earth. And damn that oncologist
who said there is nothing more he could do.

Talking to My Father on the Phone During the Last Stages of Cancer

I love yous are coming more frequently now.
I still stumble on the words, but I say them.

I mean them too. *I love you.* It sounds so—
final.

He called *me*, his *hello* a weary *goodbye.* His voice
a faded sidewalk. A postcard. A wind blown umbrella.

On the driveway two birds lay dead. Like ornaments.
Perfect. Silent. The two more surprising than the dead.

My mother looks for my father in the furniture.
He wants to live for her sake, believes

she won't live long without him.
I know that she can.

He makes me laugh. Calls the social worker from Hospice
his *psycho nurse.* Says, *she left when I couldn't help* her.

His only complaint: too many pills. I think,
Better Living Through Chemistry, and about a friend's child,

when she swallowed 64. She said 32 weren't enough.
Did she try to die for *I love you?*

As he fades I wonder,
doesn't having lived imply permanence?

I'll get better, dad said. His words, feathers.

Walking Away

8/8/89: It's easy to let myself get one step ahead of a fit!
2/19/90: I want this all to be over.

From the journal of James Kerr
(who died from AIDS 9/9/90)

We ran out of gas in your mother's car.
You told me to stay put while you walked
away, your red gas can visible
for almost a mile. Your *system* failed you.

Your system that adjusted to broken
gas gauges and too little money.
Your system that allowed you to become
invisible—your word—when necessary.

Like that time at my dining room table when
your voice grew as small as that red can.
You always returned. Not like that time your lover
went out to buy a pack of Marlboros and never

came back. Left you waiting in your robe. Left you
abandoned like a flag. Left his Paul Simon album.
Then you left Detroit and all its secrets
hidden behind the beer bottles your father collected.

His hands pewter. His voice a black crow.
He sent your mother to the Bishops to beg
to be annulled from those hands.

And now you are leaving again. Not exactly
walking away. There is no annulment from AIDS.
I remember us in 1974; you said, *I want to love this life.*
We were dancing to Stairway to Heaven.

The Arboretum

8/27/90: I feel ashamed that I feel so sorry for myself—I am actually afraid that I will have to live like this for years & that would be hell—but what can I do to make myself happy? I guess I'll have to work at it.

James Kerr

That day at the Arb—pink blanket, a bottle
of Coke, your cigarettes—we climbed the grassy hill,
vista of hemlock and maple, turquoise sky.

I sat crossed legged on the edge of shade
while you lay back on your elbows in the sun
smoking a joint, your eyes locked in smiles.

We flew through that day, admired the Frisbee-catching
dogs and the reverent quiet. We didn't know
the language of AZT or Elivil, we weren't yet talking

in vowels, still able to hold to consonants.
Later you would conjure up that day, hang on it
like a piece of sodden wood not yet ready to go down.

And Then This

8/18/90: Let the diarrhea begin & the world can go to hell.
James Kerr

I go to the word
laugh
when I think of you.
I see those lines,
extensions of your eyes,
that artery
in your forehead
that swells,
and the way
you throw your head back,
like praying
upwards.
I choke
on the contradiction:
AIDS.
The word's utterance
made me hate you,
for instantly I knew
you would leave me.
I tried on your absence,
threw vases and stones at it,
flung record albums
like Frisbees, watching
them smash
against trees
and God.
I burned Africa,
shot down airplanes,
damned every man
who ever kissed you.
My arms tore
from the weight
of pulling you
back to me.

Communion

3/28/90: I'm injecting Interferon in my stomach—taking the pills and DDI—
Jesus what an array.

James Kerr

Our last conversation
you said,
that all your life   you'd been *a shadow.*

Then you said,
    it is time for this to end

and shocked me
    with   *pray for me.*

I thought of our ritual of passing around the bong
on Sunday mornings, how you called it
            Morning Mass,

and the Communion I took
while attending church with you at Sacred Heart,
    surprised by the way the wafer melted in my mouth

before I returned to kneel next to your laughing face
and your eyes a bit scared for my brazen Jewish soul.

Before you slipped away from me
    I wanted to remind you

how fun it was to slide Kahlua into our coffee,
dance to Stairway to Heaven, and stay up all night

talking about God and fathers—how despite the lesions
and new words like *lesions* and *pneumatoid*

I still feel the warm blue stone of you,
and the joy that will wrap us together forever.

I am glad that your death eyes were 3000 miles away,
that it was your mother who was there to look into them,
telling you to let go, and I am sorry that it was not me.

I'm thinking,
maybe I will lie and say that
   I held the hand of my best friend as he died from AIDS,

which I do—only, it isn't a lie.

Section III

*I asked of everything
if it had
something more...*

     —Pablo Neruda

Redemption on Bus 18—
Bat Yam to Tel Aviv

Buses bully, bulge, breathe
intoxicated with intention,
rule the streets insolent and noisy.

A small rise from the street to the sidewalk
implanted with Hebrew letters reads:
   To the Mother and Child.

There is a purpose here not
born of Puritan beliefs,
    predestination and maps,
       it is more
desperate, more immediate,
a constant raising of community.

A bus driver rounds narrow curves of ancient roads,
stops to say hello to a friend on a moped,
sticks his hand out the window and asks him
to make change.

The mystics associate numbers
with purpose—give language to them.

Bus 18
as in the union of Hebrew letters
     meaning—*life.*

As in the latest bombing.

These people come from a diaspora.
I know none who crave return to the shtetl
or the mean streets of Europe.

Passengers offer help to a mother,
pass her baby buggy up the aisle.
There is nothing exceptional on their faces,

each hand an offering,
a renewal, a belief in numbers.

Detroit

Sunday women in blue feathered hats
and men in polished shoes, full of glory
and promise, eat Cajun at Fishbones.

Men who wash the windows
of General Motors,
who build faith on broken porches

and dance in barbecue voices
at summer picnics. They speak
in Jit and Jive, their cadence

like the hymnal breath of the radiator.
These women work the hallways at Grace
Hospital. Those men's hands press

the levers in factories left to perish
along Woodward.
Disillusioned by covenants,

the Diego Rivera mural offers
no alternative. The number of cars
produced each minute has slowed

like traffic on the Chrysler Freeway
where that huge tire
casts shade over their backyards.

Eastern Market

It wasn't the weekend. The parking lots were empty
of SUV's. A seller of flowers told us go to Vivio's
get yourselves a Bloody Mary and call it a day.

Instead, we ate sandwiches at Hambones,
temporarily married ourselves to the spires and windows,
truck after truck of produce, alleys, garbage cans. Rinks of concrete.

We snuck a beggar two bucks.

You told stories about playing third base, your father
dying one New Year's Eve, a ball game at Tiger Stadium
rather than the prom.

We admire the old men—they've accomplished something
just by living long. Like the guy in the cap that reads #1 Dad.
I asked him if he is. *She tells me I am.* I think, luck. I think
hers as much as his.

At the corner of Rivard and Erskine we imagine your father's
scrap yard now given over to grass and poplar. If we had time
we would dance there. We would search for remnants.

Corners

At six I took
a frayed blanket
behind the blue
chair covered
in unforgiving plastic,
next to the heating
duct in my mother's
living room.
I looked for her
in empty corners,
behind the familiar
smell of synthetic,
against the warm
touch of the furnace.
On the telephone
her voice hummed
in a language
I could not understand,
but imagined
told the truth.
I was six
and already understood.

Blink

Sometimes you can't tell
> if an enemy is really a friend
> > or a friend an enemy.

> Let's say

illusion
> > as in speed,
> > as in airplane
> when viewed from below,

> or the flight
> > of carrion birds.

You could say
> *rival* or *foe,*
> > I think Melanie trusted Scarlet.

Don't you?
> Flowers open themselves up
> > to fickle bees.

It isn't a mistake.

Rosabelle

Growing up I wanted to be a little black girl
with woven braids sticking out in all directions
and white teeth against luscious chocolate skin.
I wanted to be the child of Rosabelle,

hugged and kissed, soothed by strong Pinesol hands.
Joy to rest my head gently on her huge behind
while she stood on soft linoleum washing
my mother's dishes, humming her gospel songs.

Rosabelle sashayed her massive bulk toward me,
her white uniform starched and always clean.
Ain't nobody as picky about theys food as you, child.
To the *child* I attached a silent *my*.

Weekends she disappeared, returned to her real home,
to her real family I unknowingly robbed,
to some mysterious place in her concealed world.

Rosabelle stopped coming when the buses stopped running.

"No Kidding...You Play Too"

a painting by Lori Faye Bock

A rust colored cat, waxed and indifferent,
saunters across black and white piano keys
at B flat and F sharp.

Even discordance
          has its appeal.

A blue vase with orange poppies
rests on the edge
against a wall the color of the moon.

Outside, robins hold conventions,
let one another know that they are needed,
their voices the chords of desire.

This morning a friend told me that he admires me
and needs me. I repeat that ten times

so I can believe it.

He talks in chimes that make me want
to stay, maybe pick up that cat by its soft belly,
nuzzle its neck, tell it, *good boy*.

Capitalism South Carolina

A lawn sign across from the two story T. rex
and plastic Diplodocus at Jurassic Golf
on Highway 17, reads, *Jesus lives here.*

Jesus lives across from a miniature golf course
in South Carolina. The sign, professionally prepared
in perfect Times New Roman, makes me wonder

should we stop and visit?

It is the year of the Golden Pig,
the alignment of the loyal and naïve swine
with profit, making the Chinese anxious

to create polite and fortunate babies.
Ten turkey vultures covet the garbage bin
at Hog Heaven Barbecue. A brochure on my lap

says that in the 17th century this land was granted
by King George to any man
who would grow a product England could use.

Now a yellow Lockheed PV-2 Harpoon airplane
totters upon a styrofoam mountain next to a cascading
falls at May Day Golf, as though crashing in South Carolina

with a set of golf clubs would be paradise. At each street light,
submerged killer whales, 40 foot volcanoes, dragons,
viking ships, smoking turrets, creepy kitchie aliens,

and in Michelangelo's Creation of Adam,
God looks an awful lot like Elvis in a tiki hat.
We tour a plantation. I'm embarassed to be there.

Among its production, cotton, pecans, and bricks.
One plantation, 9000 bricks a day.
We were once slaves, we say every Passover,

and now we are free. My father says, *responsibility.*
He says, *never forget.* He says, *today we lean
in our seats because we can.*

In Charleston, descendents of slaves
sell sweetgrass baskets along Market Street.
In the harbor Fort Sumter floats like a lump of styrofoam.

Eve

His voice brushed against me
like fox's fur.

His hands—strong, sagacious.
I am blamed for something

I know nothing about,
bravely breaking

no rules when I fell in love.
I had no way of knowing

that the story would be blurred—
it was *he* who beguiled *me*

with appetite for knowledge
and an untamed touch.

Yes, It's a Love Poem

This place with its absence
of color. A gray barn. Snow.
A forest of leafless trees.

And then,

a red cardinal
touching vagrant silence.
A steady *chip, chip, chip.*

The Love Poems of Anne Sexton

I like to look at your underlining,
your annotations in the margins
too much,   too much.

Dog-eared pages reveal you.
You wrote:
to the goodbye, to our love, you'll see.

I come to this book of poetry to inhale
the words you breathed,
wear the same shock of red.

I once knew a drunk
who smiled all the time,
agreeably numb. Yet

I imagined when he was alone
his hands shook, milking the last drop
of yesterday's bottle. In his refrigerator

a jar of mayonnaise and a lump
of yellow cheese. We talked about it
yesterday, the idea of being underlined,

like finches as yellow as lemon meringue,
the swing of Jackie Robinson,
or when you draw me in shades of flesh and green.

Welfare in America

She is forced to live on the trains.
A husband who left, and took the boys,
her mother with whom she can only fight.

A satchel full of police reports robs
her of the right to be angry. She is judged
insane. They take away her welfare,

give her $300.00 a month and call it *disability*.
The shelters are for the invisible and the rats,
so each day she buys a rail pass and a meal.

I saw her face in the window as the train pulled out.
She leaned her head against the glass,
then closed her eyes.

Row Boat

She would have been sixteen this year,
or he. Our hands would have held
a slippery grip, a wet oar.
              Knowing about *leavings*

we would resent the implications
of a license. Instead,

my father reminds me of the time he took me
out in a row boat, we caught sunfish,

how my mother stood on the shore
cursing the dark clouds,
              cursing my father's hands

that took us further from her
                   and made us small.

How inconsistent his love was,
coming in moments
of good reception, like seasons,

like sun that emerges rather than shines.
That child wasn't the only
one we lost,

the sloughing of cells,
tiny lives that spontaneously abort.

Maybe we didn't want this enough,
this chance to worry about boats
and clouds. Hands.

Another Field

Yes, I too
want

another field
on a summer

day—a blanket
our skin

water

the motion
and rhythm

of bees.

About the Author

Joy Gaines-Friedler has a Bachelor of Arts degree in English and History. Her poetry is widely published and has won numerous awards including first place in the 2006 *Litchfield Review* contest for a series of poems based on the journal of her friend Jim who died from AIDS. Her work has also been published in *The Driftwood Review*, *MARGIE*, *The Pebble Lake Review*, *RATTLE*, *Swallow the Moon*, and other literary journals. She is currently an MFA student at Ashland University in Ohio. In addition to working in classrooms at Oakland Community College as an Academic Literacy Para-professional and a CRLA certified tutor, she is running poetry workshops for young adults at the Common Ground Sanctuary for Families in Crisis.

Other Recent Titles from Mayapple Press:

Jane Piirto, *Saunas*, 2008
Paper, 100 pp, $15.95 plus s&h
ISBN 978-0932412-645
Joel Thomas Katz, *Away*, 2008
Paper, 42 pp, $12.95 plus s&h
ISBN 978-0932412-638
Tenea D. Johnson, *Starting Friction*, 2008
Paper, 38 pp, $12.95 plus s&h
ISBN 978-0932412-621
Brian Aldiss, *The Prehistory of Mind*, 2008
Paper, 76 pp, $14.95 plus s&h
ISBN 978-0932412-614
Andy Christ, *Philip and the Poet*, 2008
Paper, 26 pp, $12.95 plus s&h
ISBN 978-0932412-607
Jayne Pupek, *Forms of Intercession*, 2008
Paper, 102 pp, $15.95 plus s&h
ISBN 978-0932412-591
Elizabeth Kerlikowske, *Dominant Hand*, 2008
Paper, 64 pp, $14.95 plus s&h
ISBN 978-0932412-584
Marilyn Jurich, *Defying the Eye Chart*, 2008
Paper, 120 pp, $15.95 plus s&h
ISBN 978-0932412-577
Patricia McNair, *Taking Notice*, 2007
Paper, 60 pp, $14.95 plus s&h
ISBN 978-0932412-560
James Owens, *Frost Lights a Thin Flame*, 2007
Paper, 48 pp, $13.95 plus s&h
ISBN 978-0932412-553
Chris Green, *The Sky Over Walgreens*, 2007
Paper, 78 pp, $14.95 plus s&h
ISBN 978-0932412-546
Mariela Griffor, *HOUSE*, 2007
Paper, 50 pp, $14.95 plus s&h
ISBN 978-0932412-539

For a complete catalog of Mayapple Press publications, please visit our website at *www.mayapplepress.com*. Books can be ordered direct from our website with secure on-line payment using PayPal, or by mail (check or money order). Or order through your local bookseller.